MYTHOLOGICAL STORIES

OF LORD KRISHNA AND RAMA

BRATESH KUMAR SINGH

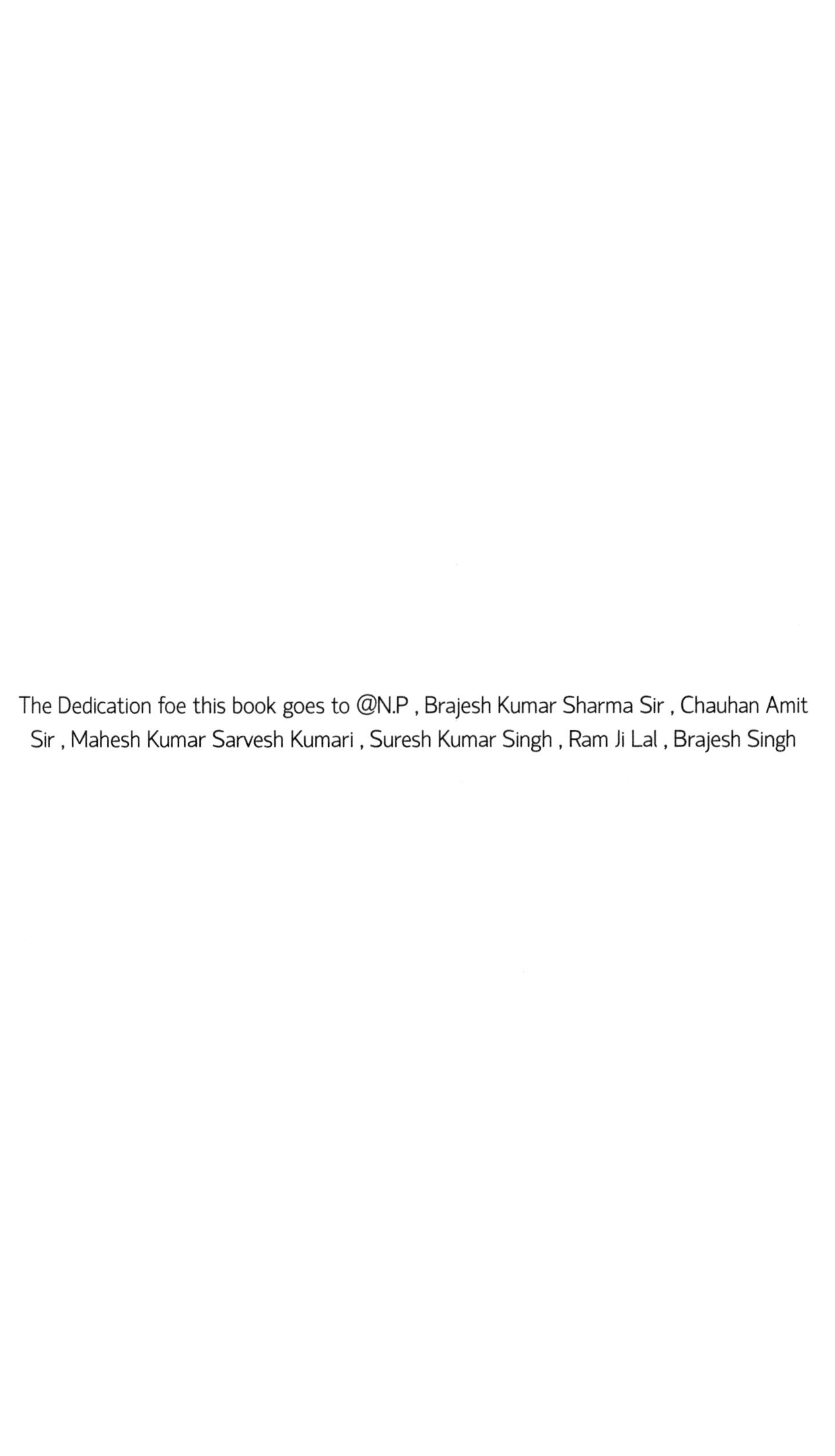

The Dedication foe this book goes to @N.P , Brajesh Kumar Sharma Sir , Chauhan Amit Sir , Mahesh Kumar Sarvesh Kumari , Suresh Kumar Singh , Ram Ji Lal , Brajesh Singh

Contents

CHAPTER ONE

Lord Krishna

In India , in the modern day state of Uttar Pradesh stands a little town near the river Yamuna. it is known as - Mathura, a holy city. it is the birthplace of Lord Krishna. Nearly 5,000 years ago, Mathura was under the rule of a tyrannical king named Kamsa. Kamsa was so greedy and cunning that he not even spared his father Ugrasena; having imprisoned him kamsa declared himself to be the King of Mathura. Ugrasena was a nice ruler, and Kamsa was just the opposite. It was a trying time for the commoners of Mathura to put up with Kamsa's extravagance and unfair rule. above all this, Kamsa locked his horns time and again with the rulers of the Yadu dynasty which led to frequent wars and troubled the peace-loving citizens of Mathura.

But soon a happy news came. Crown princess Devaki was getting married to King Vasudev of the Yadus. The Mathura citizens welcomed the wedding, for it surely meant that Kamsa's frequent wars with the Yadu dynasty would come to an end.

Soon the much-awaited day arrived. Mathura wore a festive look. Everyone was in festive spirits. Even the usually desolate citizens of Mathura were looking happy. and that was a great thing to see, since the people of Mathura did not smile often. How cold they, with such an awful king like Kamsa to guide them.

Soon, Devaki was married to King Vasudev. Kamsa, cunning as he was, thought, "Now, Vasudev's kingdom is as good as mine".

After the wedding, he decided to drive the royal couple home himself to shower on them a kingly courtesy as was prevalent in those days. But it so happened that as soon as Kamsa took the reins of the wedding chariot, a divine voice thundered from the sky," Evil Kamsa, you don't know it. But know now that by giving Devaki's hand to Vasudev, you have signed your own death warrant. The eighth son born to Vasudev and Devaki will kill you!"

Hearing this, Kamsa froze with fear. But then he became angry. He immediately thought of killing Devaki for he thought, "How can a child be born when the mother is dead?" So he drew out his sword and raised it to kill Devaki.

King Vasudev was horrified at this cruelty and fell on his knees. "O Kamsa.." he begged, "...please don't kill your sister. I shall personally surrender to you all the children she gives birth to, so that the voice of the Oracle doesn't come true."

The evil king vacillated. "Then you will live in my palace as prisoners," he declared and Vasudev had no choice than accepting his verdict. Kamsa smiled happily. The one person he loved in the whole wide world was his sister and he decided to spare her life. He was content at the thought that the situation was under his control. After all, he was not going to let her children live, was he?

Kamsa confined Devaki and her husband King Vasudev in the palace dungeons and kept them under constant watch. Every time Devaki gave birth to a child in the dungeons, Kamsa destroyed the child. In this manner, he killed seven children born to Devaki. He turned a deaf ear to all the heart- rending cries of his sister.

Nine years passed before Devaki got child for the eighth time. Kamsa, troubled by the fear of his possible death, lost his appetite and slept poorly at night. But he waited for the birth of his nemesis with murderous thoughts.

In the palace dungeons, Vasudev was trying his best to console his wife, but Devaki was terrified." My eighth child will be born in a day," she wailed. "And my cruel brother will kill this one too. Oh mighty Gods, please save my child!"

The night soon ended and the next day arrived. Devaki spent most of the day in tears. Dusk gave way to a terrible night as had not been seen earlier in Mathura. It seemed that the whole world understood Devaki's mind and joined her in mourning for the unborn child. The winds howled angrily and skies seemed to have split apart to pour wrathful rains.

Suddenly there was pin drop silence. And then it was broken by the sound of the cry of a divine child. It was of the eighth child, a son, born to Queen Devaki at midnight in the prison.

As soon the child was born, the prison was filled with a dazzling, blinding light. Devaki fainted at the sight and Vasudev was mesmerized. The light converged into a sphere and the same voice of the Oracle that scared Kamsa, now spoke to Vasudev:

" Take this child across the River Yamuna to the Gokul kingdom, ruled by your friend King Nanda. His wife Queen Yashoda has just given birth to a daughter. Exchange your son for this girl child and return to the prison immediately, before anyone comes to know about the birth of this child."

Without a word, he new father picked up his son to follow the Oracle's advice. He felt grieved to separate the newborn child from his mother but he knew that there was no other way he could save his son.

Vasudev also felt very doubtful. There were a hundred soldiers waiting outside. And it was a dark, fearsome night. How could he go out, unnoticed and unscathed?

But what he saw astonished him greatly. All his questions were answered one by one. As he approached the gate with the child in his arms, the prison doors opened automatically. He came out slowly to find to his utter surprise that all the guards were in a state of hypnotic sleep.

Vasudev left Mathura and soon approached the banks of the Yamuna river. The river seemed to be boiling white and seething with anger, due to fierce winds and rain. It looked alive and ready to devour the first person to set foot in it!

The Father looked at his the face of his infant child and hesitated in doubt. As if the river sensed his fear, the boiling subsided. But he had to proceed nonetheless. Then a miracle happened. As soon as the feet of Lord immersed in the river, the flow became normal and Yamuna made way for the Lord. To his amazement, Vasudev saw a huge black snake raising its head from the water behind him. He was scared out of his wits at first, but soon realized that it meant no harm when he saw the serpent positioning its hood like an umbrella to save the new born baby from rain. This snake was none other than Sheshnag, the Snake-God, who is known to be the roofing canopy of Lord Vishnu. It is mentioned in the texts that Krishna was the eighth incarnation of Lord Vishnu.

Vasudev did not delay any further and proceeded in waist-deep water with much difficulty. But in the end, not entirely believing his eyes, Vasudev was able to cross the opposite bank of the river safely and entered the village of Gokul.

It was past midnight and the people of Gokul were fast asleep. Thus, Vasudev had no trouble in entering the palace of king Nanda, for the palace doors were, as always, wide open. Nanda, unlike Kamsa, was a fair king and the people under his reign didn't fear for intruders or thieves in the night.

Vasudev, by this time, had some idea that his child is really someone special, it was a divine child. All his fears vanished for he understood that when he has come this far, he will surely be able to complete the rest of his journey. And that was what happened.

In no time, Vasudev reached his friend's palace. Treading softly, Vasudev entered queen Yashoda's quarters. She was sleeping peacefully in her bed and her baby girl beside her was awake, staring at the door. It was almost as if she was expecting him to come!

Vasudev scooped Yashoda's baby girl in his other arm and placed his son in the empty space next to Yashoda. With tears in his eyes, Vasudev kissed his son's forehead. "Goodbye, my son," he whispered. Then, without looking back, he left Gokul with Nanda's daughter in his arms.

With Sheshnag assisting him like before, Vasudev returned to the prison with the girl-child. He entered his dark cell and laid the baby by Devaki's side. As soon as the child felt the hard floor on her back, she opened her mouth and cried lustily.

Claannnk!!! The prison doors closed. The guards suddenly awoke from their sleep and became aware that a baby was born. They rushed to Kamsa to deliver him the news. The eighth child, slayer of Kamsa, was born!

The evil King was both pleased and afraid to hear of the birth of his nephew. He was pleased that he could finally kill the eighth child of his sister and he was also afraid that he might not be able to do so.

But putting away all his fears, he rushed to the palace dungeons to execute the child who was said to be his slayer. He reached the dungeons in great anger. The palace guards trembled at his enraged face. Kamsa entered the cell where his sister and her husband lived for the past nine years.

"Where is he?" he roared at the now-awake Devaki. "Where's my slayer?"

Devaki had regained her consciousness only after Vasudev switched the babies and so, she thought that her eighth child was a daughter. She appealed to her brother, "O Kamsa, my brother- my eighth child is a girl, and not the son that the Oracle warned you about. How can she harm you? There is no way she can. Please let your only niece live!"

Kamsa, as always, ignored her cries. He loved his life more than anything else in the world. Love for his life had clouded his common sense and he forgot the Oracle's warning about his slayer being a boy. In blind rage, Kamsa snatched the baby girl from Devaki's lap, and hurled the child against the prison wall.

But this time the baby did not die; instead, she flew up and for a second remained suspended in the air to the utter amazement of everyone present there. Then the prison was filled once again with a blinding light. Kamsa covered his face from the intensity of the light. As the light subsided, they realised that the child had changed into a ferocious Goddess!

She rose above Kamsa's head as the eight-armed form of Goddess Durga.

Dressed in shining garments and dazzling jewels, she looked terrible and divine at the same time.

The Goddess looked in contempt and pity at the bewildered Kamsa. She said, "Foolish Kamsa, there is no force on Heaven and earth that can kill me. So how can you, wretched creature? You even if you could, you would have gained nothing by killing me. For your slayer is already born! He is now well and alive in a safe place. And one day, he will come in search of you and kill you! You can’t resist him, no matter how hard you try!"

Saying so, she disappeared, leaving behind a terror-stricken Kamsa. Kamsa felt humiliated by the turn of events. In his confusion, he freed Vasudev and Devaki from prison.

Vasudev then narrated what happened on that night to his wife. Devaki, though sad at her separation from her son, was happy for the baby. Both of them prayed to God that her son should not fall into the clutches of his evil uncle Kamsa.

Meanwhile, there was great rejoicing in Gokul. The cowherd tribes of Gokul were smiling from ear to ear. A new baby boy was born to their loved King Nanda ! The streets were swept clean and the houses were decorated with colors, streamers and fragrant flowers. The whole place wore a festive look.

Everyone in the household of King Nanda was in a joyous mood. Nanda named the child Krishna. Everybody in Gokul danced with joy and flocked to Nanda’s house to see the baby boy and to offer gifts.

But it did not escape anyone’s notice that the child was like no ordinary child. His skin had a dark - blue color as is seen in a cloud filled with water during the monsoon season. His eyes twinkled merrily. He never cried and always had a smile for everyone.

Yashoda felt very proud. "Ah my son!" she crooned lovingly at Little Krishna . “my cute little son! You are surely going to be pampered and spoiled by us!”.

In this way was born Lord Krishna, the supreme God who is the creator of everyone. He was born to save everyone from the terrible tyrants like Kamsa. In his boyhood, he became the cynosure of all eyes- he won the hearts of all men and women, wherever he went. And with his brother Balaram, he later went back to Mathura and killed Kamsa.

CHAPTER TWO

Snake Kalia

It was a peaceful day in the woods. Now and then, a gentle wind blew through the fresh, green leaves of the majestic trees as if, playing merrily with them. Cuckoo birds chirped cheerfully on the branches of the huge peepal trees. Butterflies chased each other merrily and little crickets were jumping here and there. Mother Nature seemed to be laughing and enjoying the frolics of her children.

"Sssssss...." here we come!!!" suddenly hissed an evil voice, destroying the mirth and merriment all around.

Many-hooded Kalia and his brood slowly emerged from their hiding place. They were venomous beings who poisoned the very ground they slithered on. As they moved now, the grass under them turned black and the trees they passed lost their colour.
Kalia surveyed the landscape before him. "What better place to stay with my family?" he thought and grinned.

"Halt!" he ordered his family. "This is our new home!"

"No!" cried the wind, "Don't do this". "I can't breathe!" lamented a shocked peepal tree. Even the cuckoo birds on the tree branches just reeled over and died, as the air around the area turned toxic.

And so the eastern part of the Yamuna River, next to the village of Brindavan, began to slowly die.

The morning sun shone over Brindavan. It was like any other day. Everyone went about their usual business. The village primarily consisted of the cowherd tribes. They were going out to graze their cows in the nearby fields and vales. Suddenly somebody screamed in village chief Nanda's home. Everyone present nearby rushed to the place. But no one could enter inside. There were anxious whispering among the crowd that gathered outside Nanda's home. Who was it?

It was Yashoda, Nanda's wife. She sat on the bed, her body shaking in fear.

"What happened, Yashoda?" Nanda asked in worry.

"Oh dear, I had an awful dream, “shuddered Yashoda at the thought of it. "A giant snake had coiled his enormous body around our little Krishna....and...oh my God!"

"It's just a dream, Yashoda". Nanda tried to calm his wife. But Yashoda was not pacified. "I need to see if my son is all right... Krishna! My son...where are you?" she called out.

Soon, she heard the pitter-patter of a child's footsteps outside her room. Little Krishna peeked inside.

"What is it, mother?" he asked.

"Krishna, you should not go out anywhere today, do you understand?" Yashoda said gently, without wishing to alarm her son.

Krishna lingered there for sometime. Then he smiled mysteriously. It seemed to Yashoda as if he had some designs in his mind that is beyond any mortal understanding. Then, ignoring his mother's words, he ran out of his home.

"Krishna! Kishan... my son! Come back...please."

Krishna ran fast in the streets of Brindavan and arrived at the lakeside hideout where his friends welcomed him. Then they started playing with a ball.

After some time, they became tired and climbed on a tree to rest. There was a tree house on the top of it. Krishna and his friends had specially made it for their adventures. But the tiny tree was not strong enough to support so many children and it groaned under their weight. Krishna felt bad. "I wish we had a bigger tree to build a tree house. We seem to be crushing this one!"

" I know where the biggest tree in Brindavan is," said Kusela, one of his closest friends. " I would have built a tree-house on top of it. But my father said we should never go there."
"We must!" said Krishna merrily and ran towards the eastern direction. "I want to build a better treetop hideout. And I need your help. Will you please come with me?"

Krishna was loved by all his friends, so what choice did they have than to follow him?

Soon Krishna and his friends arrived at the eastern part of the Brindavan forests. But they were shocked at what they saw there. The place looked... ghostly!

On the exterior, the place looked bright enough. The lake had plenty of water and there was even a waterfall nearby. But only when the children went near they saw the changes.

The water had a bluish colour. But the grass around the lake was not green anymore. It had turned black. There was a huge tree overlooking the lake, but it was on the verge of dying. It had no leaves and its branches were all blackened. It seemed as if the whole place was damned; cursed by some monstrous evil.There was an eerie silence all about the place.

"I do not like this place," whined one of his friends." I do not like the place" he repeated, "we should not be here at all! My father will be angry if he comes to know about it."

Krishna looked thoughtfully at the lake for some moments. Then he turned to his friends. "Well then, now that we're here, let's at least play ball!" he said and grabbed the ball. He threw it at Kusela, who was unable to catch it properly and let it slip into the lake. The ball disappeared into the waters with a soft plop.

"Let me get it," said Krishna and before his friends could stop him he jumped inside the strange waters!

Krishna went under the bluish waters of Yamuna. On the shore, his friends yelled in
terror but the boy raised his head and shouted back:

"Don't worry, I'll soon be back with the ball!"

The water felt too cold and Krishna's skin tingled uncomfortably. But he ignored the feeling.

Krishna swam lower and found the plants all burnt and bent as if they were drenched in acid. It saddened him to see the underwater plants dead and black. He looked around to find out the one responsible for it.

As his feet touched the bottom, he could see skeletons of small sea animals and fishes lying on the riverbed. An uncanny silence reigned over the whole place. It seemed to be the kingdom of Death.

Suddenly a strange sound caught Krishna's ears.It seemed like a hissing sound.

"Whoever did this is still here," thought Krishna.

As if agreeing with him, a huge snake sliding out of his sea hole. It was Kalia. It was truly terrible to see his large body slithering in the water. Baring his many hoods, he hissed again and faced the little boy.

The snake-King was surprised but also pleased to see Krishna. "Hmmm, what do we have here?" he asked mockingly.

"Food!" shouted his family in chorus, who were standing behind him.

"Yessssss..." Kalia hissed in wicked tones. "We do not get to taste humans often! And you look like a pretty morsel..."

Without finishing his words, Kalia lunged at Krishna. The boy, who had been expecting such a move, deftly jumped back and hid behind a rock. But Kalia moved at a lightning speed and caught him. He coiled round Krishna and started to crush his body. Krishna, who was rather enjoying the fight, twisted his body and slipped out.

Kalia was stunned. It was impossible. How could this mere boy slip out of his grasp so easily?. Nobody, no matter how big or small, had ever escaped from his deadly hold. For the first time in his life did Kalia ever experience such a phenomenon.

Krishna, meanwhile, jumped over the rock and crouched low. He was in a playful mood and he decided to tease the evil snake.

Had he known who his opponent is, Kalia would never have dared to try to devour Krishna. Krishna was, in reality, a divine child. He was an incarnation of the Absolute, the almighty God. He had come to the earth to reward the good and punish the wicked.

But Kalia did not know this and he was hell- bent on having Krishna as his lunch.

As the snake came around the rock to catch him, Krishna ran over to the other side. The next few minutes were spent in hide and seek until, tired, Kalia lost his patience.

"You boy! Why don't you face me like a man instead of dancing like a girl?" he snarled at Krishna.

"Oh, I haven't even started dancing yet!" laughed Krishna. "But since you are asking, let me show you how I really dance..."

Saying so, Krishna quickly climbed over the rock and jumped on the snake's enormous hood. He firmly placed his foot on the snake's sensitive head and started to dance.

And what a dance it was!

The whole lake started to tremble as Krishna danced. The lake anemones and the burnt sea plants started to shake. It seemed as if they nodded their. heads together in ecstasy over Kalia's plight. Even the fishes left alive stood still and watched him dancing over Kalia's head.

"Hey you! Stop dancing on my head, will you?" Kalia screamed out in pain.

Krishna stopped dancing and slid lower near Kalia's face. He rained blows on his head and climbed on his head to dance again.

Kalia grew truly afraid. Now he felt surely that the little boy was no ordinary child. The thud of Krishna's feet felt like the bong! Bong! Of a great hammer on his head. As Krishna danced with more and more vigour, the snake felt his life slowly being pushed out of his body.

Kalia's wives were quick to predict Kalia's fate. "Oh, divine child, please don't kill our husband!" they begged him.

"I will let him live if all of you promise to leave this place forever," answered Krishna.

"But we are so safe in here!" wailed Kalia. "If we go out now, Garuda the giant eagle would surely have us as his breakfast!"

"Go to Ramnaka, the snake-kingdom," promised Krishna. "You and your family will not be attacked by any bird or beast till you reach there. That's my promise to you.. Now off you go!!"

Meanwhille, Krishna's friends ran back to Nanda's home and informed him about Krishna's underwater search for the ball.

"He has gone under water for nearly an hour..." cried Kusela, "... and hasn't returned since."

Yashoda broke into tears." I had told him..." cried he," I had warned him not to go anywhere... why didn't he listen? Oh my Krishna, my Kanhaiya... what will I do you?"

Nanda too was very much scared. He called aloud for the other Gopalas. All the village-folk rushed and followed their chief. Soon Nanda, Yasodha and everybody from the village found themselves on the blackened woods of Yamuna.

There was no sign of the little boy, anywhere. Only a deathly silence prevailed everywhere.

"Krishna... my son. Where are you?" cried Nanda, "come out! Please!"

Suddenly the waters of the lake bubbled and rose above the tallest tree in the woods. The Gopalas moved back and all of them looked in awe and fear as Krishna came out, dancing on top of a huge snake!

The snake bent his head in respect as Krishna landed on the shore. Yasodha and Nanda rushed to embrace him.

Content with Krishna's promise, Kalia gathered his brood and left Yamuna that very day. True to what Krishna said, neither birds nor beasts attacked the snake family on their way to Ramnaka. Their journey was safe and sound.

The river regained its old richness and Krishna built his tree house on the now-green tree overlooking the lake. His status was higher than ever in the eyes of all his friends. All the boys understood that Krishna was no ordinary child. Tale of his antics spread far and wide.

But none of them seemed to have any effect on the little god, who seemed content at stealing butter from his mother's kitchen and enjoying it. His eyes twinkled mischievously and his thoughts dwelled on things beyond the realms of human understanding.

CHAPTER THREE

Kansa

"Your eighth son is alive! His name is Krishna and he's in Brindavan!" said Kansa in great anger. His sister Devaki and her husband Vasudev trembled before his terrible face.

"You two have tricked me for long," continued Kansa. "But not any more. Now I will slay that kid and then, I will slay you two! I had freed you two. But now I will send you back to prison. You'll remain there until your death."

With this thundering declaration, he ordered his soldiers to arrest the couple and put them behind bars in the royal prison.

Nine years of their lives had been spent behind the bars. Now the discovery of the survival of their child again led them back to prison. The tearful couple
comforted each other and waited for that day when the tyrannical king would be slain by their son.

It was many years now since the Oracle had warned Kansa that his sister Devaki's eighth child would kill him. After destroying her seven sons, Kansa had released his sister and her husband Vasudev when the eighth child turned out to be a daughter.

But now, it was revealed that his nephew was alive and well in Brindavan; Kansa again imprisoned Devaki and her husband and returned to his private chambers.

"Kootaka!" growled Kansa in his thundering voice. "Where is Keshi? It has been two days since I send him to kill that kid. Where the hell is he?"

"Keshi... was killed by Krishna, My Lord," the first minister shuddered in fear even as he replied, for he knew well the wrath of the King.

"Whattttttttt!!!" roared Kansa. "My favourite servant Keshi? Dead? But how can that be? Is that boy so powerful?" he asked Kootaka in fear and fury.

"Yes my Lord, he is...he is... so! Indeed!" babbled the minister." He seems to be blessed with magical powers from birth, my Lord. We now know that it is impossible to kill Krishna by ordinary means. So we should resort to cunning and make him come to Mathura. "

A terrible fear had slowly creeped into Kansa's mind. He had always had the nagging fear that the words of the Oracle may, somehow, come true and that he may not be able to kill his nephew after all. But he was supposed to be the mighty ruler, master of all. How could he show his fear? Swallowing his fear, Kootaka continued," What is not achieved by swords can be accomplished by words. Call Akrura, your cousin, and order him to go to Brindavan and ask Krishna to come to Mathura. He is wise with words and will surely be able to please Krishna and make him come here without any doubt. The rest will be easy. Once the boy is here, we can kill him easily."

Kansa thought for a few minutes. "Yes, this might just work," he agreed and called for his cousin. He explained his plan to Akrura and sent him to Brindavan. But little did he know that Akrura was a great devotee of Krishna!

Akrura didn't waste a moment. With great anxiety, he set out for Brindavan. Once there, he immediately told Krishna of Kansa's evil intentions.

Krishna laughed. He said, "Seems like Kansa is very eager to die," he said, "He's inviting death to come to him, instead of waiting for it patiently. If that is what he wants, then let him have it. Let us all go to Mathura!"

Krishna took the blessings of his parents, who gave their consent after much hesitation. Though they knew that their sons were no ordinary mortal, the thought of any harm coming to their sons worried them greatly.

Krishna left Brindavan with Akrura and travelled to his uncles kingdom, along with Balaram, his brother. The news of Krishna's visit spread in Mathura. So everywhere there was curiosity, excitement and joy.

Meanwhile, Kansa was hatching a plan to do away with his nephew. Suddenly he had idea.

"Is the mad elephant Kuvalayapida awake?" he asked Kootaka.

"Yes, my lord." answered Kootaka. " He's safely chained but he's trying to break free."

"Then let him free in the streets!" hissed Kansa. "Let him kill the two young brothers!" he roared madly.

Kootaka, silently followed the king's order, and released the elephant in the streets, much against his wishes. For he too didn't want Krishna and Balaram to die. But the thought of the wrath of the king made him do otherwise.

As the mad Kuvalayapida was released, he started to destroy everything in his way. People screamed in fear and ran for their lives.

Suddenly, Kuvalayapida saw a blue-skinned youth standing in the middle of the main street. The youth was Krishna. The elephant rushed towards him. Just as he neared him, Krishna took his sword and cut off his trunk. The mad animal trumpeted in pain, fell down and died.

The people of Mathura were awestruck at Krishna's bravery. They yelled his name and shouted their praises aloud. The old women of the city blessed the two

brothers and the young maidens threw flowers at them.

"Jai Krishna! Jai Balaram!" cried the people, " Cheers for the two!"

"How they adore us!" exclaimed a smiling Balaram.

"Yes, but don't let it go to your head, brother. We are still surrounded by danger," cautioned Krishna.

And Krishna's prediction soon proved to be correct.

Back in the court, Kansa was full of anger. "Now the elephant is also dead. Tell me a way to kill my nephew! I will leave no stones unturned to see them dead. " he screamed at his minister.

"My Lord, you can trust Mushtika and Chanura to do the job. I think they will surely be able to kill Krishna," said Kootaka. "They are invincible warriors and they have never been beaten by any mortal till now."

"Yes!!!" agreed Kansa happily. "You're right! The demon brothers Mushtika and Chanura will surely kill my nephew!"

Kansa immediately sent word to them. They came out of their resting places and watched the two brothers walking near the arena.

""Ha ha! Are these kids going to fight us? Why, they look as puny as newborn kittens!" laughed Chanura. "Look at them! So small, so weak... we can crush them with our little finger!" cackled Mushtika.

But what happened then was what no one ever expected.

THUUNNNNNNK!!!

It was the hard blow that Mushtika felt on his head the very next moment. Balaram had attacked Mushtika, using his mighty mace. Mushtika fell down with an enormous roar of pain .He lay on the ground, writhing in agony.

"You hit my brother!!!" Chanura roared. "How dare you attack him? I will not spare you. I will kill you..." he yelled and lunged at Balaram. The next minute, he lay flat on the ground, groaning in pain. Krishna had clubbed him.

By this time, the arena was full of eager spectators who wished the two demon warriors dead.

"Oh no! They're mere boys! What can they do against these demon-like wrestlers!" a softhearted woman shook her head in despair over the impossibility of the
situation.

"Our Krishna and Balaram are divine beings, blessed by Lord Vishnu. They will surely kill them," assured another man.

Suddenly the woman shrieked, "Behind you, Krishna!"

Krishna looked behind just in time to see Chanura ready to strike him with an enormous axe. He moved fast and escaped from the axe. He bent, caught hold of Chanura's meaty legs and tugged hard. The demon lost his balance and fell down with a hard thud!

Meanwhile, back in the palace, Kansa was restless. He had waited for long and could no longer contain his impatience. "My demon warriors must have killed Krishna by now... I want to see the boy dead!" he thought greedily and rushed to the arena with a devilish grin.

But what he saw there shocked him out of its wits. What a terrible shock he got when he found his best warriors in the clutches of Krishna and Balaram!

For the first time in his life, Kansa saw Krishna and his heart almost stopped in fear and terror. His nightmares, somehow, seemed to have come true.

Krishna looked up and saw that Kansa had come to watch the fight, "Here, Uncle!" he yelled in glee. "Watch your demons die!"

Saying thus, Krishna crushed the life out of Chanura without much effort.

"And now, it is your turn to go to Hell, evil Kansa!" thundered Krishna.

Kansa felt his body freeze within his body. He felt a terrible fear at the sight of his smiling nephew advancing towards him. This was the scene that he had seen in his nightmares, night after night, for the past few years. Filled with a mortal fear for his life, Kansa tried to run away.

The people of Mathura were delighted at their evil king's terror. "Punish Kansa! Kill the tyrant for his unfair rule! "Let him not escape!" they yelled in rejoice.

Kansa ran around the arena, hoping to find a gap where he could escape. But the citizens of Mathura whom he had tormented all these years, were not in a forgiving
mood. They circled the arena, not allowing Kansa to escape from the ground. Much injustice had been borne in silence. Much tears had been shed. Much had the citizens of Mathura endured without raising a voice out of fear. At last they had the opportunity to strike back. And they relished every moment of it. The king was laughed and jeered at wherever he ran. He had no escape now.

Krishna pounced on Kansa, caught hold of his hair and pushed him to the ground. "You are no more a king. You were never fit to be a king !"he declared and
wrenched off Kansa's crown.

But the king hardly minded. All he wanted was to be left alive. Kansa tried to get up to save himself. But Krishna's hold was like the grip of Death.

"Leave me Krishna," pleaded Kansa at last, "Forgive me...please!"

"It is too late now to beg for pardon. Your time is up, wicked tyrant." roared Balaram. "It is now your time to die. Think about your dark deeds in the darkness of Hell".

"Now I'm going to crush you tighter and tighter for every sin you committed," said Krishna in anger. "This is for imprisoning my parents and making them live in a
dungeon for nine years!" he said and tightened his hold. Kansa struggled to breathe.

"This is for killing my seven brothers and countless innocent children in Mathura when I was born!" said Krishna, and tightened his hold further.

Kansa felt his lungs
exploding.

"And this is for imprisoning my grandfather and terrorising the people of Mathura for all these years!" Krishna declared and finally snapped his head. Kansa breathed
his last and fell to the ground, dead.

The skies opened and flowers were showered from the heavens. The words of the Oracle had finally come true. Kansa was killed by the eighth son of Devaki!

After a long long time could the people of Mathura could smile again. They heaved a collective sigh of joy and relief. At last, they free from the reign of the evil Kansa.

"Our task is not yet finished. We have one more duty, Balaram," reminded Krishna.

"You are right, brother." nodded Balaram in agreement.

The brothers hurried to the palace and entered the dungeons where Devaki and Vasudev were imprisoned. They opened the prison gates.

"Mother," called Krishna softly. Devaki and Vasudev could not believe their eyes. Here was their son standing before them. They were mad with joy to see their son. Devaki embraced Krishna and shed happy tears over him.

Krishna then rushed to the next cell, where he freed his grandfather Ugrasena. Ugrasena blessed him and said, "My grandson, you are now the king!"

"Yes Grandfather. But my destiny lies elsewhere,and there I must go first," replied Krishna as he prepared to leave for Brindavan.

Thus ended the tyranny of the evil Kansa. Punishment came to him late, but it was a punishment just and as terrible as his actions were.

CHAPTER FOUR

Indra and Krishna

In the country of India, there is a little town called Brindavan. It is a famous and a very holy place for it is associated with the birth of Lord Krishna. The holy God was born there 5000 years ago. He was born on the earth as an ordinary human being, to punish the wicked and protect the good.

It was the rainy season. The sun was smiling weakly behind dark clouds. Brindavan, then a charming village, was transformed into a lush heaven with healthy, greener vegetation and plenty of rains for the people. Everyone in the village was happy.

Krishna woke up with a start. It was not yet morning, but the sounds coming from the streets were loud and noisy enough to wake one up. Curious, he got up and peeked outside his window.

A crowd had gathered before his house. Several men and women were sweeping the streets clean. The roads were being decorated with garlands and lamps.
Krishna was surprised at the sight, as he had seen since his birth that in the rainy season, the villagers slept till late in the morning.

"Is it a festival today? Or is anybody getting married?" he wondered. But he couldn't remember any such occasion.

He left his home to take a bath in the river. While coming back, he saw his father Nanda overseeing the men in the streets.

"Father, what is happening on the streets?" Krishna asked his father.

"The Gopalas are preparing to celebrate a festival to worship Lord Indra," said Nanda. "This year, there has been a rainfall more generous and everybody is happy with the fertile crops. Since Indra is the God of rains, we should thank Him for being so gracious in his blessings!"

"How do you say that Lord Indra is the one who's causing rains, Father?" Krishna frowned in disagreement.

Nanda looked at his son in alarm.

"Of course it's Indra who's causing the rains, son. He is surely the reason for our good fortune. He's the God of the Clouds and he rules them... so he is the one who has blessed us with good rain this year," he replied hesitantly to his son.

"No, father!" refused Krishna firmly, "you're all mistaken. Govardhan Mountain is our real friend. More than the clouds above, the mountain in our village has helped us."

"How can you say that?" asked Nanda, looking at his son in disbilief.

"The fertile mountain sends the signals in the air and creates clouds that drift over the Brindavan and give us rains." replied Krishna. "So whom should we praise and worship? Not Indra, but Govardhan!"

Nanda and the other Gopalas at work gasped in surprise. How could Krishna dismiss Lord Indra, God of the Clouds and direct them to worship a mere mountain instead! This was the first time that they heard about such a thing.

"Yes, father," continued the boy. "Who gives us medicine in the form of magical herbs and plants? Who sends us clean water and air from the top of its peak?
"And who gives us good grass for our cows, so that they give us milk that's sweeter than honey? It is Govardhan!"

The initial surprise and doubts of the Gopalas were beginning to disappear. They now began to see Krishna's point.

"So why should we not worship the mountain?" Krishna continued. "It is wiser to give thanks to something which is right before us, rather than some deva who lives comfortably in the heavens."

Hearing Krishna's words, the Gopalas were totally convinced. They all agreed to worship Govardhan that year, instead of Lord Indra. But Nanda was apprehensive, for he feared that this shifting of loyalty might incur the wrath of God upon them.

And his fear came true. Up in the skies, Lord Indra was listening to this conversation in anger and fury. "So that little cowherd boy has stopped the celebrations in my honour!" he thought in indignation.

Lord Indra's pride was insulted by the Gopalas' decision to worship Govardhan, instead of him. In his anger, he decided to punish the people of Brindavan.

"All these years I have heard their plea and helped them to prosper. And is this what I get in return? It's time they know who the real God is here! I'll send the most dangerous rains and thunderstorms to Brindavan," he thought cruelly. "They will destroy the whole village of Brindavan. Let them see who saves them then!"

What he thought he soon realised in action. Using his divine powers, Lord Indra created clouds that seemed to be darker than the midnight sky. They looked devilish and fearsome.

"Go and destroy Brindavan!" he ordered.

And they heeded their Master's command. Without any delay, they grouped together to form a menacing army of clouds and raced towards the village where Krishna and several innocent families lived.

"This will be enough for them" thought Indra and laughed aloud.

After a delicious lunch, the people of Brindavan were dozing in their homes. Suddenly they heard a terrible sound.

Crassssssssshhhh!!!

Everybody was alarmed and came out of their homes. What they saw outside took their breath away.

It was noon in Brindavan, but nobody could say it was so. The whole village had become pitch dark. The sun was nowhere to be seen. Instead, black and terrible looking clouds had invaded the village. They enveloped the whole place in a thick mist, darkening the day, making it gloomy.

The clouds looked evil and menacing, but they stood suspended in air and didn't rain. It seemed as if the clouds were waiting for somebody, or rather, for some signal.

The people of Brindavan watched in fear and awe. They were spellbound. Nothing like this had ever happened in their lives!

Krishna heard the frightened voices of the villagers. He was curious and came out of his house. But as soon as he stepped out, there was a great roar and the black clouds poured rains over Nanda's house. It seemed as if this was what the monstrous clouds had been waiting for.

The demonic clouds seemed to have some fiendish scheme. From Nanda's house, they quickly spread themselves over the town. The dark sky seemed to open with a vengeance. Hard rain came down in torrents, flushing away the cattle and the frail huts. The mere thatched roofs were no match for the terrible downpour.

"Run! screamed a man in terror and people started to run for their lives. They ran in all directions, to save their family and belongings. But even escape seemed difficult for the Brindavan people. The hard and blinding rain lashed over their faces, as if giving slaps for some unknown offence. Nowhere could they take any shelter for nothing seemed to be strong enough against this mighty cloudburst. The innocent and helpless people wailed in the face of such a calamity. They prayed for some divine help.

But the clouds were merciless. They now had the support of blinding lightning and ear-splitting thunder.

Every now and then, lightning struck a fertile tree and destroyed it. Thunder rumbled throughout the ordeal, shaking' people's nerves and panicking them. Nanda felt helpless on seeing his people panic.

"Do you see, son? This is no ordinary rainstorm. This seems to me to be the punishment of our transgression. It is difficult to escape the wrath of Gods. That is why we worshipped Lord Indra all these years, Krishna," he said to his son gravely. "Because we decided to ignore Lord Indra this year, he's punishing us. Now, innocent people are suffering because of your idea... what to we do now?"

Krishna looked at the skies. "Ah, vain Indra!" he thought in fury. "I understand your plan. You want to teach us a lesson, don't you? But first, you need one! And soon I will crush your ego."

Thinking so, Krishna laid a reassuring arm on his father.

"First, we need to focus on making the people see reason, Father," he said and walked to the centre of the town. Using his most commanding voice, he called out:

"O people of Brindavan. Look at me. Do not run. Do not panic!"

The Gopalas looked at Krishna miserably. They had known the boy for long. They knew that he was not an ordinary mortal and possessed some mysterious powers.
But what can the boy possibly do in such a situation?

"This is all our fault!" somebody murmured. "We insulted Indra and now he's punishing us," continued another.

"Yes uncle Guran, what you say is right. This is indeed an evil plot of Lord Indra," replied Krishna, looking at the man. "But like before, Govardhan would help us once again. Come this way and I will show you how!" he declared and led them to the mountain.

Krishna looked up and smiled at the clouds. And in a blink of the eye, he lifted Govardhana Mountain, like an umbrella over the people.

People forgot to breathe. A small boy had lifted a mountain on his little finger!

Up above, Indra was bewildered. "How can a mere child lift a mountain?" he thought. He hadn't ever seen such a feat achieved by anybody, leave alone a child.

"You should have understood it by now. But you did not. Pride and arrogance has clouded your common sense, Indra!" sounded the voice of Brahma.

Lord Indra looked at the God of Creation in confusion.

"Don't you know that Krishna is a divine child?" continued Brahma. "Aren�t you aware that he�s an incarnation of Lord Vishnu? Shame on you!"

Indra was humbled and stopped the rains. As a sign of his apology, he ordered the clouds to shower rose petals from the skies. Then the applause began.

Every Gopala whooped in delight at their darling boy for his strength and wisdom. They now saw what a godly child lived amidst them. They composed songs in praise of the Lord, singing of this miraculous feat. Shouts of "Long Live brave Krishna!" seemed to echo everywhere.

And it continues even today.

Back to Mythology Main

- Friendship Day
- Good Morning Images for WhatsApp
- Moral Stories
- Benefits of Yoga for Kids
- Monthwise Calendar Wallpapers
- Singhasan Battisi
- Horror stories
- Indian Mythology stories

- School Projects
- Study in UK with Scholarship and Work Visa

Download IIT KGP 2022 Calendar on The Myth of Aryan Invasion Recovery of the Foundations. Indian Knowledge Systems

Back to Home | Stories for Kids | School Projects | Fun & Jokes | Refer This Page

In the country of India, there is a little town called Brindavan. It is a famous and a very holy place for it is associated with the birth of Lord Krishna. The holy God was born there 5000 years ago. He was born on the earth as an ordinary human being, to punish the wicked and protect the good.

It was the rainy season. The sun was smiling weakly behind dark clouds. Brindavan, then a charming village, was transformed into a lush heaven with healthy, greener vegetation and plenty of rains for the people. Everyone in the village was happy.

Krishna woke up with a start. It was not yet morning, but the sounds coming from the streets were loud and noisy enough to wake one up. Curious, he got up and peeked outside his window.

A crowd had gathered before his house. Several men and women were sweeping the streets clean. The roads were being decorated with garlands and lamps.
Krishna was surprised at the sight, as he had seen since his birth that in the rainy season, the villagers slept till late in the morning.

"Is it a festival today? Or is anybody getting married?" he wondered. But he couldn't remember any such occasion.

He left his home to take a bath in the river. While coming back, he saw his father Nanda overseeing the men in the streets.

"Father, what is happening on the streets?" Krishna asked his father.

"The Gopalas are preparing to celebrate a festival to worship Lord Indra," said Nanda. "This year, there has been a rainfall more generous and everybody is happy with the fertile crops. Since Indra is the God of rains, we should thank Him for being so gracious in his blessings!"

"How do you say that Lord Indra is the one who's causing rains, Father?" Krishna frowned in disagreement.

Nanda looked at his son in alarm.

"Of course it's Indra who's causing the rains, son. He is surely the reason for our good fortune. He's the God of the Clouds and he rules them... so he is the one who has blessed us with good rain this year," he replied hesitantly to his son.

"No, father!" refused Krishna firmly, "you're all mistaken. Govardhan Mountain is our real friend. More than the clouds above, the mountain in our village has helped us."

"How can you say that?" asked Nanda, looking at his son in disbilief.

"The fertile mountain sends the signals in the air and creates clouds that drift over the Brindavan and give us rains." replied Krishna. "So whom should we praise and worship? Not Indra, but Govardhan!"

Nanda and the other Gopalas at work gasped in surprise. How could Krishna dismiss Lord Indra, God of the Clouds and direct them to worship a mere mountain instead! This was the first time that they heard about such a thing.

"Yes, father," continued the boy. "Who gives us medicine in the form of magical herbs and plants? Who sends us clean water and air from the top of its peak?
"And who gives us good grass for our cows, so that they give us milk that's sweeter than honey? It is Govardhan!"

The initial surprise and doubts of the Gopalas were beginning to disappear. They now began to see Krishna's point.

"So why should we not worship the mountain?" Krishna continued. "It is wiser to give thanks to something which is right before us, rather than some deva who lives comfortably in the heavens."

Hearing Krishna's words, the Gopalas were totally convinced. They all agreed to worship Govardhan that year, instead of Lord Indra. But Nanda was apprehensive, for he feared that this shifting of loyalty might incur the wrath of God upon them.

And his fear came true. Up in the skies, Lord Indra was listening to this conversation in anger and fury. "So that little cowherd boy has stopped the celebrations in my honour!" he thought in indignation.

Lord Indra's pride was insulted by the Gopalas' decision to worship Govardhan, instead of him. In his anger, he decided to punish the people of Brindavan.

"All these years I have heard their plea and helped them to prosper. And is this what I get in return? It's time they know who the real God is here! I'll send the most dangerous rains and thunderstorms to Brindavan," he thought cruelly. "They will destroy the whole village of Brindavan. Let them see who saves them then!"

What he thought he soon realised in action. Using his divine powers, Lord Indra created clouds that seemed to be darker than the midnight sky. They looked devilish and fearsome.

"Go and destroy Brindavan!" he ordered.

And they heeded their Master's command. Without any delay, they grouped together to form a menacing army of clouds and raced towards the village where Krishna and several innocent families lived.

"This will be enough for them" thought Indra and laughed aloud.

After a delicious lunch, the people of Brindavan were dozing in their homes. Suddenly they heard a terrible sound.

Crasssssssssshhhh!!!

Everybody was alarmed and came out of their homes. What they saw outside took their breath away.

It was noon in Brindavan, but nobody could say it was so. The whole village had become pitch dark. The sun was nowhere to be seen. Instead, black and terrible looking clouds had invaded the village. They enveloped the whole place in a thick mist, darkening the day, making it gloomy.

The clouds looked evil and menacing, but they stood suspended in air and didn't rain. It seemed as if the clouds were waiting for somebody, or rather, for some signal.

The people of Brindavan watched in fear and awe. They were spellbound. Nothing like this had ever happened in their lives!

Krishna heard the frightened voices of the villagers. He was curious and came out of his house. But as soon as he stepped out, there was a great roar and the black clouds poured rains over Nanda's house. It seemed as if this was what the monstrous clouds had been waiting for.

The demonic clouds seemed to have some fiendish scheme. From Nanda's house, they quickly spread themselves over the town. The dark sky seemed to open with a vengeance. Hard rain came down in torrents, flushing away the cattle and the frail huts. The mere thatched roofs were no match for the terrible downpour.

"Run! screamed a man in terror and people started to run for their lives. They ran in all directions, to save their family and belongings. But even escape seemed difficult for the Brindavan people. The hard and blinding rain lashed over their faces, as if giving slaps for some unknown offence. Nowhere could they take any shelter for nothing seemed to be strong enough against this mighty cloudburst. The innocent and helpless people wailed in the face of such a calamity. They prayed for some divine help.

But the clouds were merciless. They now had the support of blinding lightning and ear-splitting thunder.

Every now and then, lightning struck a fertile tree and destroyed it. Thunder rumbled throughout the ordeal, shaking' people's nerves and panicking them. Nanda felt helpless on seeing his people panic.

"Do you see, son? This is no ordinary rainstorm. This seems to me to be the punishment of our transgression. It is difficult to escape the wrath of Gods. That is why we worshipped Lord Indra all these years, Krishna," he said to his son gravely. "Because we decided to ignore Lord Indra this year, he's punishing us. Now, innocent people are suffering because of your idea... what to we do now?"

Krishna looked at the skies. "Ah, vain Indra!" he thought in fury. "I understand your plan. You want to teach us a lesson, don't you? But first, you need one! And soon I will crush your ego."

Thinking so, Krishna laid a reassuring arm on his father.

"First, we need to focus on making the people see reason, Father," he said and walked to the centre of the town. Using his most commanding voice, he called out:

"O people of Brindavan. Look at me. Do not run. Do not panic!"

The Gopalas looked at Krishna miserably. They had known the boy for long. They knew that he was not an ordinary mortal and possessed some mysterious powers.
But what can the boy possibly do in such a situation?

"This is all our fault!" somebody murmured. "We insulted Indra and now he's punishing us," continued another.

"Yes uncle Guran, what you say is right. This is indeed an evil plot of Lord Indra," replied Krishna, looking at the man. "But like before, Govardhan would help us once again. Come this way and I will show you how!" he declared and led them to the mountain.

Krishna looked up and smiled at the clouds. And in a blink of the eye, he lifted Govardhana Mountain, like an umbrella over the people.

People forgot to breathe. A small boy had lifted a mountain on his little finger!

Up above, Indra was bewildered. "How can a mere child lift a mountain?" he thought. He hadn't ever seen such a feat achieved by anybody, leave alone a child.

"You should have understood it by now. But you did not. Pride and arrogance has clouded your common sense, Indra!" sounded the voice of Brahma.

Lord Indra looked at the God of Creation in confusion.

"Don't you know that Krishna is a divine child?" continued Brahma. "Aren�t you aware that he�s an incarnation of Lord Vishnu? Shame on you!"

Indra was humbled and stopped the rains. As a sign of his apology, he ordered the clouds to shower rose petals from the skies. Then the applause began.

Every Gopala whooped in delight at their darling boy for his strength and wisdom. They now saw what a godly child lived amidst them. They composed songs in praise of the Lord, singing of this miraculous feat. Shouts of "Long Live brave Krishna!" seemed to echo everywhere.

CHAPTER FIVE

Kansa and Putna

Kansa knew that the eighth child, according to the prophecy, would be his slayer. When the eighth child was born to Devaki, Kansa immediately arrived at the prison and snatched the baby from Devaki. This was actually the goddess Yogmaya. She laughed at Kansa for his foolishness and told him that his slayer had been born and was living in Gokul.

Kansa was furious and ordered his men to kill all children born on the same day as Krishna, but the men returned empty-handed. Finally, Kansa sent Putana, the queen of the demons, to kill Krishna. She planned to kill him by feeding him poisoned milk.

Krishna was lying in the cot in the courtyard Nanda's house. Putana assumed the form of a beautiful maiden and happened to be passing by. When she saw Krishna, she asked for permission to pick him up. She offered her breast to feed him and Krishna sucked the life out from her.

CHAPTER SIX

Kansa is Killed

Finally, Kansa decided to get Canura and Mustika, the famous wrestlers to kill Krishna and Balarama. Thousands of people gathered to watch the brothers fight the powerful wrestlers. Krishna and Balarama appeared fragile before the stout wrestlers, but they pushed, punched, and twisted their bodies with such force that Canura and Mustika died on the spot within minutes.

As the crowds cheered, Kansa, in a fit of rage, ordered the two brothers to be driven out of the city. Hearing Kansa speak this way, Krishna became very angry. He turned to Kansa and ran towards him. Kansa drew a sword and attacked Krishna. Fighting empty-handed, Krishna grabbed Kansa's long hair and stuck him with his mighty fist. Kansa at once fell and died. The crowds roared and celebrated as they saw the cruel king breathe his last.

CHAPTER SEVEN

Lord Ram is Born

King Dasaratha was unhappy because he had no heir to the throne. One day, Sage Vashistha, asked the king to perform the Ashvamedha yajana.

Meanwhile, Ravana, had acquired the boon of immortality from Brahma, and was creating havoc in heaven and on earth. The gods appealed to Vishnu to get rid of him.

While the yajna was going on, a magnificent figure arose and gave King Dasaratha a bowl of payasam, a rice pudding prepared as an offering to the gods.

The king gave the payasam to each of his three wives - Kausalya, Kaikeyi, and Sumitra.

Soon, the queens gave birth to beautiful boys. Lord Rama, the reincarnation of Vishnu, was born to Kausalya; Bharat to Kaikeyi; and Laxmana and Shatrughna to Sumitra.

CHAPTER EIGHT

Shree Ram and Lakshman

King Dasaratha's children were taught by the great sage Vashistha. Though all four were very bright, Rama was the best and most adored.

One day Sage Vishmitra came to King Dasaratha and told him that two demons named Mareecha and a Subahu were troubling the sages. He asked King Dasaratha to send his brave sons, Rama and Laxmana, to fight the two demons and enable the sages to perform their rituals. King Dasaratha sent Rama and Laxmana with the sage to the forest of Dandka.

The brothers kept a strict watch outside the sage's hut while the rituals was going on. Five days past peacefully but on the morning of the sixth day a thunderous roar was heard. All looked up to see an approaching army of demons clouding the skies. Rama aimed Mareecha, and hurled into the sea. The next shot at Subahu, killed the monster immediately. The two brothers then easily defeated the rest of the army.

CHAPTER NINE

Lord Rama and the Squirrel

ama wanted to cross the bridge to Lanka in order to save Sita from Ravana's clutches. He sat down to pray to the sea god. The sea god, Samudra, arose from the depths of the sea and told Rama to build a bridge across the sea.

All the monkeys got busy building the bridge by placing boulders. A tiny squirrel was watching everything from his burrow. He decided to help Rama. He began picking sand and scattered twigs and scurried back and forth from the shore to the sea. Little by little the squirrel had gathered an entire heap.

Rama noticed the dedication of this tiny creature. Picking it up on his palm, he warmly stroked the animal with his three fingers. Since then, it is believed that squirrels have three lines on their body.

CHAPTER TEN

Shree Ram Crosses Sea

To cross the sea and go to Lanka, Rama shot his arrows through the water. The sea god, Samudra appeared before Rama. With hands folded he said that if the sea dried, the natural balance would be affected. He suggested that Rama should consult Nal, Vishwakarma's able son and a soldier in Sugreeva's army, to construct a bridge. Accordingly Nal laid out a plan for the construction. All the monkeys got together to build the bridge. Large trees, bamboos, huge rocks, and a lot of sand were used to construct the platform.

When Nal finished building the bridge, all the gods including Samudra came too see it. They admired his work and showered petals on it. Once it was constructed, Samudra assured Rama that he would keep his waters stable when the monkey brigade crossed the bridge. The sea became still . Then it was time for Rama and the huge army of monkeys to cross the bridge.

Sugreeva said to Rama,"Let Hanuman and Angad carry you and Laxmana on their backs, while the rest of the army walks on." Agreeing to Sugreeva's suggestion, Rama and Laxmana climbed Hanuman and Angad's sturdy shoulders. Once Rama and Laxmana were carried across, the huge battalion of monkeys followed. Some jumped, some screamed, while others danced as they marched on bravely towards Lanka.

CHAPTER ELEVEN

Lord Ram Killed Sambhuk

One day, an old Brahmin walked into Rama's court with the deadbody of his son. He was crying and started blaming Rama for the death of his five-year-old son. The Brahmin said that he had never committed a sin in his life and couldn't understand why his son had died at such an early age. He was convinced that his son must have died as a result of some sins committed by Rama.

Rama was very sad and summoned Sage Vashistha. The sage told him that a man called Shambuk, an untouchable, was doing a very powerful tapasya, which he was not permitted to do. If he was punished, the little boy would come back to life. Rama immediately left in search of Shambuk.

Finally, Rama found Shambuk praying near a river in the forest. When Shambuk revealed his identity, Rama took out his sword and cut Shambuk's head off and the little boy became alive again.

CHAPTER TWELVE

Lord Ram kills Khara

Bruished, Shurpanakha rushed to her brothers Khara and Dushana. She narrated the incident and asked them to take revenge. Khara and Dushana were demon kings. Seeing Shurpanakha's plight, they became very angry. Meanwhile, Rama sensing some trouble, asked Laxmana to escort Sita to a secure place. He got ready with his bow and arrow. Khara and Dushana arrived with strong army of elephants, horse drawn chariots, and soldiers. The battle began. The enemies charged from all directions and Rama hit back with his powerful arrows . He destroyed the entire army. Finally, with one final shot he knocked down Khara, Dushana , and their friend Trisara . Meanwhile , one demon called Akampana, who survived the attack , rushed to Lanka to inform Ravana.

CHAPTER THIRTEEN

Shree Ram meets Sita

Rama sent Hanuman to fetch Sita from Vatika.

When she arrived before Rama, tears of joy rolled down her cheeks and she ran to embrace him, but Rama stopped her.

Rama too was delighted to meet Sita after so long. He told her that he and Laxmana had risked their lives to save her. He said, "I have risked everything to save you. For the past one year you have lived in another man's house. You have to prove your purity."

Hearing this Sita asked Laxmana to set up her funeral pyre. Laxmana looked at Rama, but the latter was unmoved. He had no choice but to obey Sita's order.

As the flames rose up, Sita mounted the pyre, but miraculously did not burn. Rama and Sita were reunited again and all the gods in the heavens blessed them.

CHAPTER FOURTEEN

Lord Ram Returns To Ayodhya

After killing Ravana and rescuing Sita, Rama, Laxmana made preparations for their return to Ayodhya. They sat in a flying chariot and bid farewell to the army of monkeys. However, the monkeys insisted on accompanying Rama so he decided to take them along. Meanwhile, Rama sent Hanuman to Ayodhya to let everyone know that they were all returning.

The entire city of Ayodhya was brightly lit and people thronged the roads with garlands in their hands to welcome Rama. As soon as the flying chariot touched the ground, Bharata rushed forward to touch Rama and Sita's feet. Rama, Laxmana, and Sita met their mothers, Kaushalya, Sumitra, and Kaikeyi, who was very ashamed of her deeds.

Sage Vashishta ordered arrangements for Rama's coronation to be made, Finally, Rama sat on the throne and sage Vashistha crowned him the king of Ayodhya and the other sages also blessed him. The people of Ayodhya rejoiced.

CHAPTER FIFTEEN

Luv and Kush

After the battle with Ravana, following Rama's instructions, Laxmana left Sita on the banks of the river Ganga. The pupils of sage Valmiki saw Sita crying and told their guru. Sage Valmiki realised that the woman was actually Sita and brought her to his ashram. From then on, Sita lived at the ashram of sage Valmiki under his care. A few months later, she gave birth to twins. All the people at the ashram were happy because they had all grown very fond of Sita. Sage Valmiki names the two boys. Luv and Kush. The twins stayed at the ashram and Sage Valmiki educated them.

Sage Valmiki knew that the boys would grow up and be as strong, wise, and intelligent as their father, Rama. He taught them archery and soon Luv and Kush became good warriors.

CHAPTER SIXTEEN

Luv Kush Fights Lakhman

Luv and Kush defeated Shatrughana's army and refused to return the sacred horse. Hearing the news, Rama sent Laxmana to Valmiki's ashram to bring back the horse. However, Luv and Kush were stubborn and refused to part with the horse without a fight. Under Valmiki's guidance, Luv and Kush had become expert at archery and so were not afraid of Laxmana. A fight ensued between them and Laxmana. Kush promptly took his bow and arrow and sent an arrow toward Laxmana. Laxmana was furious and soon a fight between Laxmana on one hand, and Luv and Kush on the other, started.

Laxmana was very impressed with the strength and might of the two brothers. Luv and Kush shot many arrows at Laxmana and finally Laxmana was defeated and fell to the ground. Rama was shocked when he heard of Laxmana's fate. He summoned Bharata and told him to go to Valmiki's ashram with Hanuman.

CHAPTER SEVENTEEN

Shree Ram meets with Luv and Kush

When Rama came to know about the defeat of Bharata and ... at the hands of Luv and Kush, he decided to go to Sage Valmiki's ashram himself and meet the boys. When he reached the ashram and met Luv and Kush, he asked them who they were. Luv replied that they were the children of Vanadevi, as Sita was known in the ashram. They said that sage Valmiki had educated them.

As soon as Rama heard this, he realised that these brave young boys were his own sons. In the meantime, Luv and Kush started shooting arrows at Rama and his army. Just then, Sage Valmiki appeared. He told the boys that Rama was actually their father. Rama hugged his children and wept with joy.

Printed by Libri Plureos GmbH in Hamburg,
Germany